A Character Building Book™

Learning About Forgiveness from the Life of
Nelson Mandela

Jeanne Strazzabosco

The Rosen Publishing Group's
PowerKids Press™
New York

Published in 1996 by The Rosen Publishing Group, Inc.
29 East 21st Street, New York, NY 10010

First Edition

Book design: Erin McKenna

Photo credits: Cover © Archive Photos; p. 7 © Mark D. Phillips/Photoreporters; pp. 8, 16 © Ryan Williams/International Stock; all other photos © AP/Wide World Photos.

Strazzabosco, Jeanne.
    Learning about forgiveness from the life of Nelson Mandela / Jeanne Strazzabosco.
        p.   cm. — (A character building book)
    Includes index.
    Summary: A brief biography of the South African civil rights worker and president who serves as an example of forgiveness.
        ISBN 0-8239-2413-0
        1. Mandela, Nelson, 1918– —Juvenile literature. 2. Presidents—South Africa—Biography—Juvenile literature. 3. Civil rights workers—South Africa—Biography—Juvenile literature. 4. South Africa—Politics and government—1948– —Juvenile literature. 5. Forgiveness—Case studies—Juvenile literature. [1. Mandela, Nelson, 1918– . 2. Presidents—South Africa. 3. Civil rights workers. 4. South Africa—Politics and government. 5. Blacks—South Africa—Biography. 6. Forgiveness.] I. title. II. Series.
DT1974.S77 1996
968.06'4'092—dc20   96-20208
                                                                                                         CIP
                                                                                                         AC

Manufactured in the United States of America

Table of Contents

Nelson Rolihlahla Mandela

Nelson Mandela was born in 1918 in **Tvezo** (tveh-ZOH), South Africa. His parents named him **Rolihlahla** (roh-lih-SHLAH-shlah). This was a traditional name of the Tembu people. It means "to stir up trouble." The name was perfect. Nelson Rolihlahla Mandela spent his life "stirring up trouble" against **racist** (RAY-sist) South African rulers. A small group of white people had all the power. Nelson fought for **equal** (EE-kwul) rights for black South Africans. In South Africa, black people had no freedom, few rights, and little power to change these things.

◀ *Nelson has spent most of his life fighting for change in South Africa.*

Apartheid

In 1948 the white South African government began **apartheid** (ah-PART-hayt), or rule by separation. Many white South Africans believed that whites were better than blacks. Under apartheid, black South Africans had to live in townships. These were in poor areas of the country and outside of the towns. They could not vote. They could not travel without carrying a **passbook** (PASS-book). Black children were given poor education. Most blacks had very little money. These conditions angered Nelson. He wanted to change the way things were.

Most black South Africans were forced to live in poor townships outside of the white towns and cities. This township is called Soweto. ▶

STAMP OUT
APARTHEID
DIVEST NOW
ALLIANCE AGAINST WOMEN'S OPPRESSION
LOCAL 420
AFSCME

Poor Living Conditions

When he was older, Nelson wanted to move to the beautiful city of Johannesburg. But because he was black, he was forced to live outside the city. The neighborhood for blacks had no plumbing, electricity, or garbage collection. Many people lived in shacks made of wood or sheet metal. People were often sick or hungry. When Nelson saw the terrible living conditions of his people, he decided to fight the system. He was accepted to college. He worked hard in college to become a lawyer. He wanted to represent his people.

◀ *Many people, both black and white, disliked the way black South Africans were treated. Some of these people protested that things should be changed.*

The ANC

In 1944, Nelson joined the African National Congress (ANC). The ANC was a **political** (poh-LIH-tih-kul) party formed by blacks to fight for their freedom and rights. Within the ANC, Nelson formed the African National Youth League. This group organized black teens and taught them how to help in the fight for equality. Nelson organized **strikes** (STRYKS), wrote articles against apartheid, and gave speeches to thousands of people. He became a leader.

Nelson is still a member of the ANC. ▶

Banned

Nelson's actions worried the South African government. The government issued a **ban** (BAN) on him. He was not allowed to go to meetings. He was not allowed to leave the area of Johannesburg. It was difficult to take part in ANC activities while he was banned. Nelson went into hiding. The government could not find him. Only people he trusted knew where he was. For a year, he continued his fight. Disguised, he traveled to other African countries and to Great Britain to get support for the fight against apartheid.

The ban on Nelson kept him from speaking at meetings like this one. Today, as President of South Africa, he is free to speak to whomever he chooses.

Arrested

The white government refused to listen to blacks. Nelson saw that words alone would not bring freedom or change unfair laws. In 1962, Nelson formed a group called Spear of the Nation. Members were armed and taught how to fight.

In August 1962, Nelson was arrested. He was charged with **sabotage** (SA-buh-toj) and **treason** (TREE-zun). He was found guilty and sentenced to life in prison. He was not allowed to receive visitors or letters. The government knew he was a threat.

Nelson was arrested for fighting for freedom for all. This is a photograph of Nelson one ▶ year before he was arrested.

International Support

Many black and white South Africans protested Nelson's imprisonment. They also continued to fight for democracy. South African police tried to stop all protests. They often beat or shot protesters. Hundreds of people were killed over the years.

People all over the world heard about Nelson's imprisonment. Many people didn't agree with the system of apartheid. They decided to support Nelson and try to help end apartheid. Many countries refused to do business with South Africa.

◀ *People in South Africa and around the world protested Nelson's imprisonment.*

The Right to Be Angry

Nearly 25 years later, the South African president, F. W. de Klerk, visited Nelson in prison. De Klerk knew that apartheid was wrong. He wanted to find a way to end it peacefully. He wanted to work with Nelson because he knew that many black South Africans would listen to him. Many white South Africans were afraid that if black South Africans were equal, they would take revenge on whites. Nelson knew that black South Africans had reason to be angry. But he believed it was important to change South Africa peacefully.

F. W. de Klerk and Nelson Mandela worked together to find a better way to run South Africa. ▶

Freedom

Nelson was angry about the way he and all black South Africans had been treated. But he put his anger aside. He was able to forgive those wrongs. Because he forgave these things, he and de Klerk were able to work together. In 1990, Nelson was released from prison. After 27 years, Nelson was free. Many people in South Africa and around the world celebrated. When Nelson was released from prison, he told black South Africans to work for peaceful change. He told them to look to the future, not the past. He told them to forgive.

◀ *Nelson told the people of South Africa to forgive those who ran the government of apartheid.*

Working Together

Nelson and de Klerk worked hard to change the South African government. They worked for a new **constitution** (kon-stih-TOO-shun) giving black South Africans their freedom and the right to vote. In 1991, the system of apartheid ended. South Africa was a **democracy** (dee-MOK-ruh-see). Nelson and de Klerk both received the 1993 Nobel Peace Prize.

A presidential election was held in 1994. Millions of black South Africans voted for the first time in their lives. Nelson was elected president. Nelson Mandela is known all over the world as a symbol of change and forgiveness.

Glossary

apartheid (ah-PART-hayt) Governmental system of separateness.

ban (BAN) To forbid someone to speak in public or meet with more than one person.

constitution (kon-stih-TOO-shun) Rules by which a country is run.

democracy (dee-MOK-ruh-see) Government that is run by the people and for the people.

equal (EE-kwul) The same in value.

passbook (PASS-book) Former means of identification for black South Africans.

political (poh-LIH-tih-kul) Having something to do with the government.

racist (RAY-sist) Person who judges other people based on the color of their skin.

Rolihlahla (roh-lih-SHLAH-shlah) Tembu name meaning "to stir up trouble."

sabotage (SA-buh-toj) Damage done on purpose.

strike (STRYK) When workers refuse to work until their demands are met.

treason (TREE-zun) Acting against your country.

Tvezo (tveh-ZOH) Village in South Africa.

Index

DATE DUE

FEB 2 8 '99			
JUN 0 4 2008 - ILL#42535769 VLD			
GAYLORD			PRINTED IN U.S.A.